ADRIFT AT SEA

A Vietnamese Boy's Story of Survival

by Marsha Forchuk Skrypuch
with Tuan Ho

Art by Brian Deines

pajamapress

First published in the United States and Canada in 2016

www.pajamapress.ca   info@pajamapress.ca

Canada Council   Conseil des arts
for the Arts   du Canada

ONTARIO ARTS COUNCIL
CONSEIL DES ARTS DE L'ONTARIO
un Ontario government agency
un organisme du gouvernement de l'Ontario

Canadä

The publisher gratefully acknowledges the support of the Canada Council for the Arts and the Ontario
Arts Council for its publishing program. We acknowledge the financial support of the Government of
Canada through the Canada Book Fund (CBF) for our publishing activities.

Library and Archives Canada Cataloguing in Publication

Skrypuch, Marsha Forchuk, 1954-, author
     Adrift at sea : a Vietnamese boy's story of survival / by
Marsha Forchuk Skrypuch with Tuan Ho ; art by Brian
Deines. -- First edition.

ISBN 978-1-77278-005-5 (hardback)

     1. Ho, Tuan, 1975- --Juvenile literature. 2. Vietnamese
Canadians--Biography--Juvenile literature. 3. Boat people--
Vietnam--Biography--Juvenile literature. 4. Political refugees--
Vietnam--Biography--Juvenile literature. 5. Political refugees--
Canada--Biography--Juvenile literature. I. Ho, Tuan, 1975-,
author II. Deines, Brian, illustrator III. Title.

FC106.V53S57 2016   j971'.004959220092   C2016-902501-2

Publisher Cataloging-in-Publication Data (U.S.)

Names: Skrypuch, Marsha Forchuk, author. | Ho, Tuan, author. | Deines, Brian, illustrator.
Title: Adrift at sea : a Vietnamese boy's story of survival / by Marsha Forchuk Skrypuch with Tuan Ho ;
art by Brian Deines.
Description: Toronto, Ontario Canada : Pajama Press, 2016. | Summary: "Tuan and his family survive
bullets, a broken motor, and a leaking boat in the long days they spend at sea after fleeing Vietnam. A
true story as told to the author by Tuan Ho. Includes family photographs and a historical note about the
Vietnamese refugee crisis"-- Provided by publisher.
Identifiers: ISBN 978-1-77278-005-5 (hardcover)
Subjects: LCSH: Ho, Tuan -- Juvenile literature. | Refugees -- Vietnam -- Biography – Juvenile literature.
| Vietnam War, 1961-1975--Refugees--Juvenile literature. | BISAC: JUVENILE NONFICTION
/ Social Topics / Emigration & Immigration. | JUVENILE NONFICTION / Biography &
Autobiography / Historical. | JUVENILE NONFICTION / People & Places / Asia.
Classification: LCC DS559.914.H6S579 |DDC 959.704092 – dc23

Original art created with oil paint on canvas
Cover and book design—Rebecca Bender
Photographs: Saigon City Hall–© Pierre Nordique; Vietnamese Refugees–Public Domain;
All other photos courtesy of the Ho family

Manufactured by Qualibre Inc./Print Plus
Printed in China

Pajama Press Inc.
181 Carlaw Ave. Suite 207 Toronto, Ontario Canada, M4M 2S1

Distributed in Canada by UTP Distribution
5201 Dufferin Street Toronto, Ontario Canada, M3H 5T8

Distributed in the U.S. by Ingram Publisher Services
1 Ingram Blvd. La Vergne, TN 37086, USA

▲ Clockwise from bottom right,
Tuan, Lan, Linh, Loan in Saskatoon,
Saskatchewan, 1982

◀ Tuan's mother (top), his sisters, Lan (left) and Loan (right), and five-year-old Tuan, 1980

Van and her grandmother, Khuong, at the airport before their flight to Canada. Top, from left to right: Family friend and grandmother. Bottom from left to right: Tuan's cousins, Thao and Chau, and his sister Van, 1985 ▶

For those whose quest is freedom—M.S.

To all Vietnamese refugees: those who made it and those who did not. To my Aunty Nghia and late Uncle Tri and my cousins Diana and Amanda, who kept us company on our journey. To Aunty Bang and Uncle Hai for taking care of Vanessa. And to my mom and dad for their courage, love, and tireless effort to give us all a better life.—T.H.

For Minou—B.D.

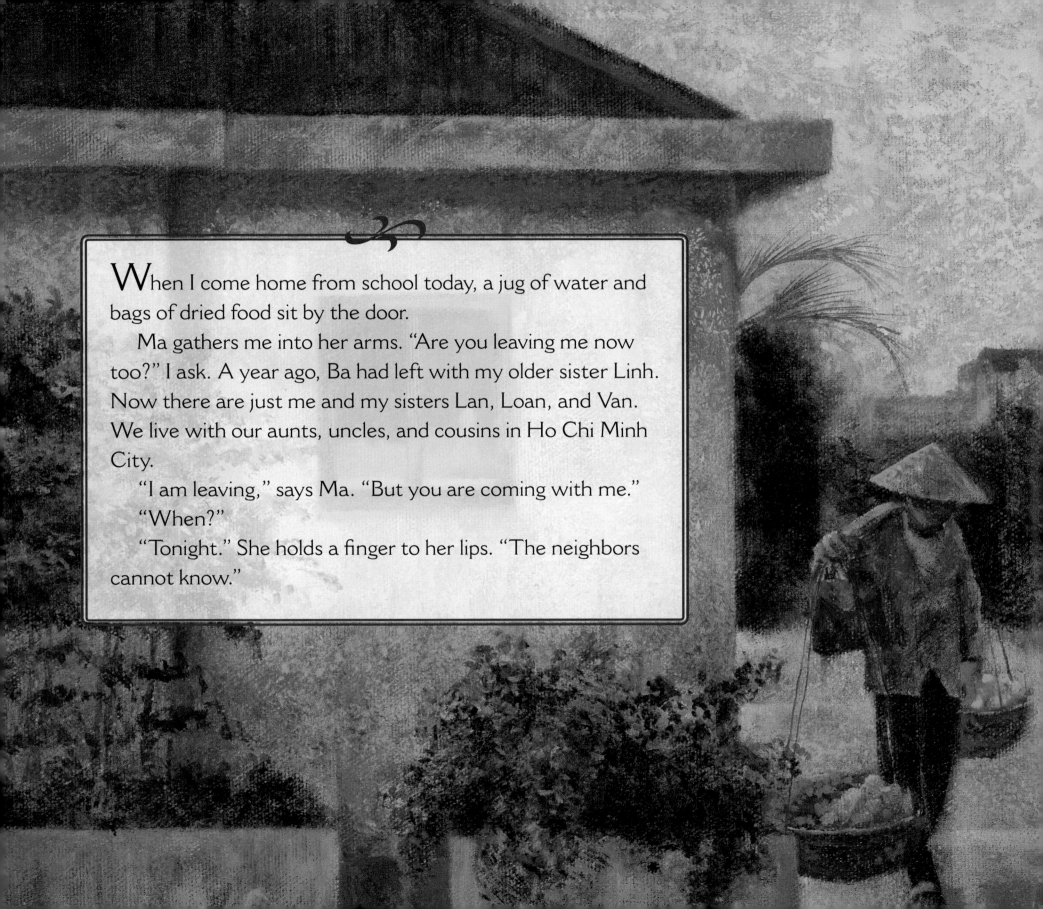

When I come home from school today, a jug of water and bags of dried food sit by the door.

Ma gathers me into her arms. "Are you leaving me now too?" I ask. A year ago, Ba had left with my older sister Linh. Now there are just me and my sisters Lan, Loan, and Van. We live with our aunts, uncles, and cousins in Ho Chi Minh City.

"I am leaving," says Ma. "But you are coming with me."

"When?"

"Tonight." She holds a finger to her lips. "The neighbors cannot know."

That night I toss in bed. What will my future be? I hold Ba's cap to my face. The scent reminds me of his last words. "Be brave, Tuan."

Ma touches my shoulder and I jolt awake.

I dress in layers and tiptoe down the stairs. Lan, Loan, and Ma are there. Aunt Nghia waits with two of her children, but not little Thao. Aunt Bang and Uncle Hai are not there. Nor are their children. Uncle Tri is not there either.

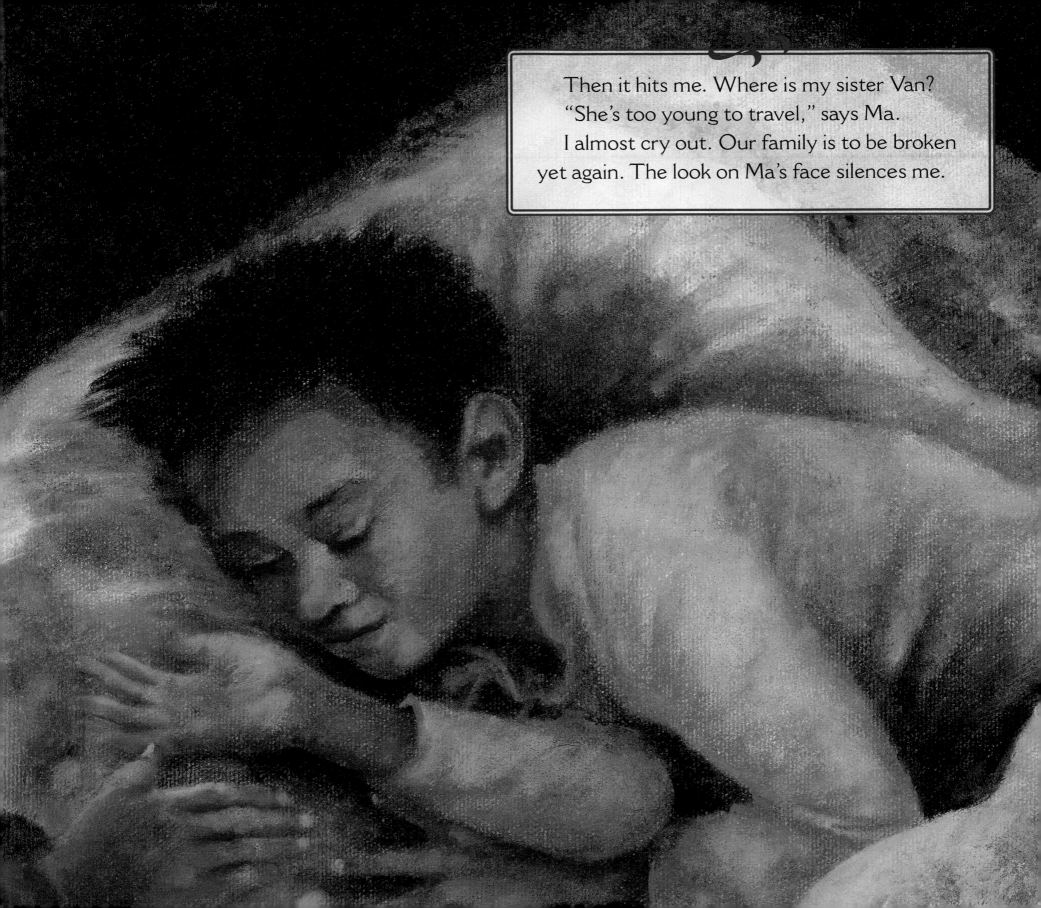

Then it hits me. Where is my sister Van?
"She's too young to travel," says Ma.
I almost cry out. Our family is to be broken
yet again. The look on Ma's face silences me.

We slip outside. A truck pulls up. We climb in and hold onto each other as it careens over bumps and potholes. It stops.

"Get out before they catch me,"
says the driver.
 We hide among bushes close to
the water until skiffs appear.
 "Now," says Ma.

I jump over rocks and bushes, running to the boats. Guns fire. One bullet pierces a clump of dirt by my foot. I stumble and roll, head over heels. I get up and keep running.

Soldiers shout. My heart pounds.

Loan scrabbles onto a skiff, pulling me in. Strangers crawl in beside us. Where are Ma and Lan? My cousins? Aunt? The boatman pushes off.

"Help me." It's Ma, clutching onto the side, knee-deep in water. We pull her in.

Bullets fly past our heads. We duck. The motor kicks over and we speed away.

When the gunshots subside, I realize the horrible truth: the rest of my family is lost. We travel in terrified silence.

The sea is empty for long minutes but
now a large fishing boat appears.

They lower a plank. I walk across,
looking down into the moonlit inky sea,
numb with sorrow.

Another skiff. Lan! Aunt Nghia beside
her. Cousins too. Our family is found.

After they board, another skiff appears, and I count heads as these people walk the plank to our larger boat. We are sixty. The captain starts the motor and we speed away.

It's hard to find a place to sit, but finally we huddle together, clutching hands and falling asleep to the lullaby of slapping waves and the growl of the motor.

Next morning, the sun burns down onto my face and my throat is like paper. What I would love is a tall, cool glass of milk, but I know that's not possible.

"Ma, can I have some water?"

She pours a trickle into the cap of the jug and hands it to me. I gulp it down.

"More please."

"This trip lasts four days," she says. "This is all the water we have."

I take off one of my shirts and put it over my head to block out the sun. I drift in and out of sleep, thinking of water, dreaming of milk. My lips crack and my skin peels.

On the second day, our boat springs a leak. I wish I could drink the water that laps around my feet, but it's full of salt.

Ma and Nghia take turns bailing. It's hard work and few offer to help. Don't they realize our boat could sink?

The captain gives them a bottle of water in thanks. We hide this treasure in our bags.

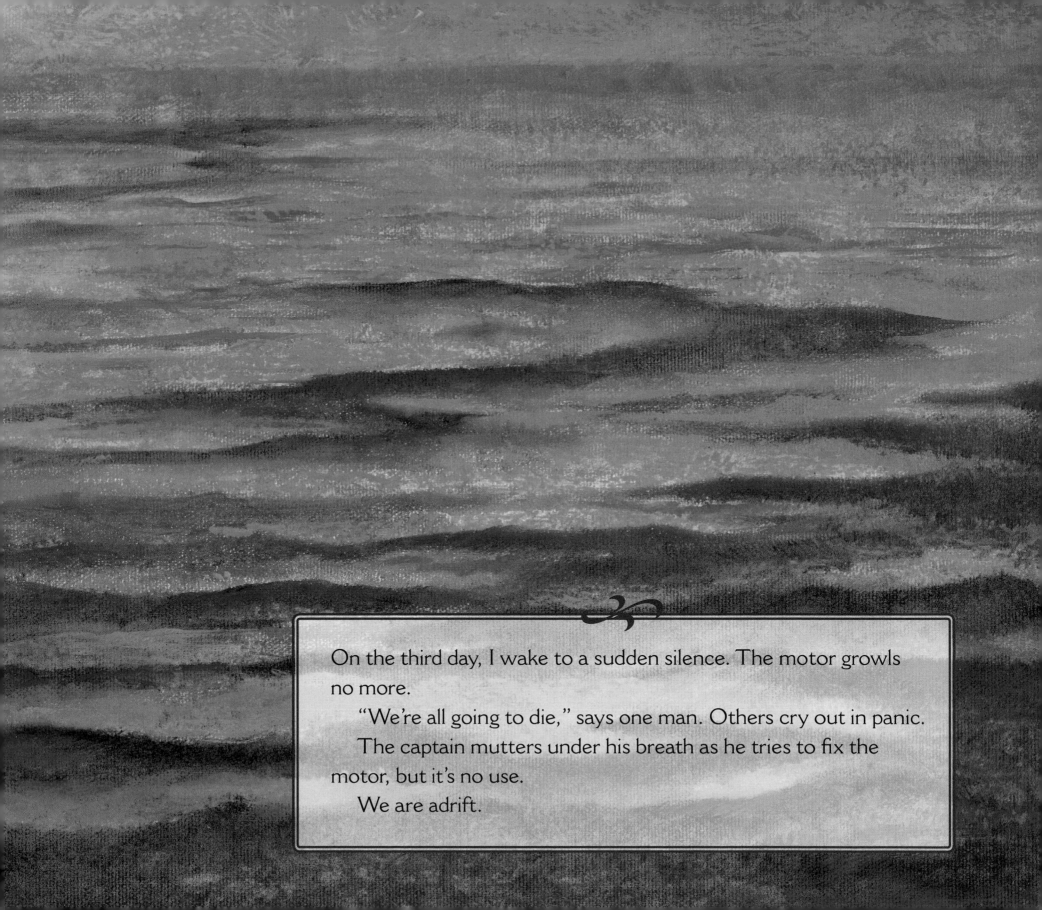

On the third day, I wake to a sudden silence. The motor growls no more.

"We're all going to die," says one man. Others cry out in panic.

The captain mutters under his breath as he tries to fix the motor, but it's no use.

We are adrift.

On the fifth day, I spy a boat, drifting like we are.

That night, as I sleep, that other boat is suddenly bright with fire.
I wake up to the commotion on our boat.

"They think we're a rescue ship," says the captain. "They've lit a
fire to get our attention."

The flames in the distance suddenly envelop that boat. It
overturns. The flames and boat are swallowed by the sea.

We sixty stare in silent horror, but there is nothing that we can
do to help.

Will this be our fate as well?

When I close my eyes, I see that burning boat. I cannot sleep. I
go to help Ma bail water.

As she empties her pail over the side, she gasps. I stand
on my tiptoes to look. Just below the surface are many
dolphins. "It's a sign, Tuan," Ma says.
Her words confuse me, but I am comforted too.

On day six I see something in the distance that seems too big to be a ship. It looks like a bright, white light. As it gets closer, the captain cries out, "It's American. An aircraft carrier!"

"Help us!" I whisper. My throat is too dry to cry out.

The massive ship looms above our tiny boat. The American
sailors wave. When we are close enough, we see their
smiles. A sailor tethers us. They lower a rope ladder.

We climb up one after another. When it is my turn, I am
afraid I will be too weak to hold onto the ropes. But I can't
give up now. I climb. A sailor lifts me off from the topmost
rung and sets me on the deck. He smiles and talks, but I
don't understand.

He gives me a tall glass filled with milk. I gulp it down.
The cold wetness soothes my parched tongue and throat.
I hold up my glass, hoping for more.

The sailor beams.
He gives me another,
and another.
I smile.
We are safe.

Between 1955 and 1975, the Vietnam War was fought between North Vietnam (supported by the Soviet Union) and South Vietnam. Starting in 1965, the United States sent over 553,000 troops to help its South Vietnamese allies. 58,220 of them lost their lives before the war ended in 1975, with the communist forces overtaking the South Vietnamese capital of Saigon, now known as Ho Chi Minh City.

The new communist government punished those who did not share their beliefs. Thousands who were labeled "enemies of the people" were executed, while others had their homes confiscated and were forced to live in the jungle. The new government made it impossible for shop owners to continue doing business, and it also targeted some minorities with particularly harsh treatment.

It is a testament to how horrible life was that so many thousands of Vietnamese were willing to risk their lives for a chance to escape. For twenty years following the Fall of Saigon, people tried to escape Vietnam any way they could.

The only way out was by sea, and those who could afford it would bribe government officials in order to get their documents and a boat. Those who didn't have the money had to sneak away secretly and without travel papers. Rich or poor, they all ended up in boats not made for long travel on open water.

In 1979, the number of "boat people" increased dramatically. Large boats filled with refugees tried to land in Southeast Asian countries, but were denied permission until Western countries agreed to resettle them. At the same time that these large boats were looking for a place to land, thousands of tiny boats started out on treacherous journeys of escape. The people in these small boats faced storms and pirates, and risked dying of thirst or hunger.

◄ Map showing the journey of Tuan and his family

— Escape route from Vietnam
— Rescue by aircraft carrier and subsequent route to Bidong refugee camp
— Two months later, inland route to Kuala Lumpur refugee camp where they spent three months before immigrating to North America

Saigon City Hall, 1968 ▼

◄ An overcrowded fishing boat full of Vietnamese refugees

Tuan's father, Nam, at his job during the Vietnam War, working for the Americans as a translator ▶

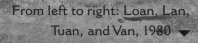

Tuan's sisters Linh (top) and
Loan (bottom) ▶

From left to right: Loan, Lan,
Tuan, and Van, 1980 ▼

Tuan's father Nam with his older
sister Linh at the Malaysian
refugee camp, 1980 ▶

Even if they survived the trip and landed in a neighboring country, they were often pushed back out to sea with no place to go.

Temporary refugee camps were set up along the shores and islands of Malaysia, Thailand, Singapore, and other neighboring countries, but they became so overcrowded that food and water had to be strictly rationed and sanitation was a problem. In June 1979, the Southeast Asian countries declared that they could not accept any more refugees.

The United Nations convened in July to deal with the humanitarian crisis. Southeast Asian countries were persuaded to continue providing temporary shelter and western countries agreed to accelerate the resettlement process. Most of the refugees ended up settling in the United States, France, Australia, and Canada.

Top from left, Loan, Linh, Tuan, Van, and Lan. Bottom from left, Phuoc, and Nam, 2016 ▼

In 1980, Tuan's mother Phuoc and his father Nam wanted to get the whole family out of Vietnam by boat together, but they realized it would be impossible because Tuan and his sisters were so young—Van was three, Tuan was five, Lan was eight, Loan was nine, and Linh was twelve. Instead, they decided that just their father, Nam, would escape with Linh. The new plan was for them to get to Canada and sponsor the rest of the family to join them later.

While Nam and Linh had a perilous journey by boat, they did ultimately get to Canada. Unfortunately, the process of sponsoring the rest of their family was slow and frustrating. Meanwhile, life in Vietnam was getting worse.

On May 19, 1981, when Tuan was six, Phuoc devised a new escape plan, taking Tuan and his two older sisters Loan and Lan by small boat, just as her husband and oldest daughter Linh had done the year before. It was a terrifying and risky journey and she made the difficult choice of leaving her youngest daughter Van behind with her sister and brother-in-law because she was afraid that Van would not survive the journey. After two days of travel and four days adrift, they were rescued by an American aircraft carrier. The U.S. navy transported them to a refugee camp on Bidong Island off the coast of Malaysia. Two and a half months later they were transferred to Kuala Lumpur, Malaysia. After three more months, the four of them joined their father and Linh in Saskatoon, Saskatchewan, on October 6, 1981.

Finally, on December 12, 1985, eight-year-old Van and her grandmother Khuong rejoined the family in Toronto, Ontario. United at last, the whole family went on to build rich lives in their new country. Today, Tuan Ho and his wife Edae Lam (who herself is the child of a boat family) live north of Toronto and are the parents of two young daughters, Madelyn, and Emily. Tuan completed his bachelor of science (honours) degree at the University of Toronto in 1998 and then completed his master's degree in physiotherapy at the University of Vermont in 2003. Tuan also completed his contemporary medical acupuncture training at McMaster University in 2009.

Tuan Ho has been a dedicated physiotherapist for the past twelve years and has recently opened up a physiotherapy clinic.

▲ Tuan and his family today: Emily, Edae, Tuan, and Madelyn